RETHINK, REBUILD & RESTORE!

---

11 Essential Principles for Changing Your Life

By R. Renee Dupree, Ph.D.

Legal & Disclaimer

The information contained in this book and its contents is not designed to replace or take the place of any form of medical or professional advice; and is not meant to replace the need for independent medical, financial, legal or other professional advice or services, as may be required. The content and information in this book has been provided for educational and entertainment purposes only.

The content and information contained in this book has been compiled from sources deemed reliable, and it is accurate to the best of the Author's knowledge, information and belief. However, the Author cannot guarantee its accuracy and validity and cannot be held liable for any errors and/or omissions. Further, changes are periodically made to this book as and when needed. Where appropriate and/or necessary, you must consult a professional (including but not limited to your doctor, attorney, financial advisor or such other professional advisor) before using any of the suggested remedies, techniques, or information in this book.

Table of Contents

Introduction

❧

Rethink, Rebuild and Restore! is a broad-reaching program of 11 principles designed for individuals who have experienced a life-changing experience and now choose to rebuild their lives. This includes:

- Individuals who have lost a job
- Anyone recovering from addiction
- Anyone who has suffered a personal betrayal or business loss
- Those who have been incarcerated and are about to transition from correctional facilities to community reentry, as well as individuals who have made the transition back to the community
- Those who are rebuilding following the loss of a loved one
- All others who have undergone tremendous upheaval and have made the decision to rebuild their lives

This multi-faceted program provides individuals with the tools, information and direction toward personal and career growth. *Rethink, Rebuild and Restore!* augments but does not replace 12-step and other recovery programs or bereavement counseling that focuses on the grieving process. The principles it outlines are a proactive effort that encourage individuals to examine their mindset, discover and engage with new information, create a sense of purpose and inclusion in their local communities, and involve businesses, government agencies, nonprofit organizations, police departments, and participants in mentoring and educational roles to work together for positive and impactful change.

The Mission

Rethink, Rebuild and Restore! provides individuals with relevant training, information, and the opportunity to lead healthy, productive lives.

The Vision

Every person who *Rethink, Rebuild and Restore!* reaches has an opportunity to access information and learn, transcend his/her past, and be embraced as a valuable, productive member of society.

The Starting Place

Rebuilding starts in your mind. Everything you do to rebuild yourself should be focused on increasing your self-esteem, knowledge, self-confidence, and abilities for a fresh, productive start. One of the biggest barriers that individuals face after any personal devastation is their mindset. A successful readjustment begins in your mind.

Dr. R. Renee Dupree, author of *Rethink, Rebuild, and Restore!* has years of professional experience in the fields of educational training, mindset training, and public speaking in the broad area of self-improvement and motivation. Dr. Dupree has written this book to inspire anyone who is ready and willing to pick up the pieces of a shattered life, help bridge gaps that may exist between those individuals and the larger community, and create a unified bond of purpose and achievement. Our successes are only measured by those weakest among us that we help to grow strong. *Rethink, Rebuild and Restore!* is a journey toward that strength and limitless achievement. Isn't it time for all of us to get on board?

It's Time to Get to Work!

Are you ready to break through the secular rules that are holding you back and finally find and follow the path toward success that you deserve? For some, this workbook may be a treacherous road into an unknown wilderness as you navigate a new understanding of how pressing challenges can be overcome and real success can be attained and enjoyed by merely changing your mindset. For others, this workbook will offer a comforting reprieve from the way the world does things and offer a refreshing way to get back on track to your dreams.

Rethink. Rebuild and Restore! is a complete guide, offering the steps necessary to change your mindset and finally achieve the contentment and success you deserve. All you have to do is start dealing with life with a different mindset and looking at the road to success through a different lens.

FOREWORD

There is a song called "if it ain't one thing it's another," Rethink, Rebuild & Restore written by Dynamic speaker and author Dr. R. Renee Dupree, Ph.D. is a book that's needed now more than ever before. The department of labor reports over twenty thousand people are losing their jobs every day. The negative impact on millions of families have been devastating.

This book is a blueprint on how to regain your life after a major setback. As a twenty-one year cancer conquer, I found each chapter inspiring, enlightening and instructive. My personal friend and business partner, Dr. R. Renee Dupree is not only the messenger; she is the message that she talks about. After going through a series of setbacks, betrayals, business loss, bankruptcy, public humiliation and the loss of her father she reinvented herself, picked up the pieces of her life and started rebuilding with a hunger that comes from deep inside.

Starting over with nothing but faith, drive and a hunger to get back on top again, Dr. R. Renee Dupree-McCoy proves in each chapter you have comeback power. Each page reminds you if "life knocks you down try and land on your back because if you can look up, you can get up."

My friend, Dr. R. Renee Dupree-McCoy has always been a motivator of people and encourages her readers to exude positivity and confidence, champion justice, fairness, and equality. Be courteous, be attentive, be responsible, operate with good character, show compassion and be sensitive to the needs, customs and positions of others. She strives to always pay it forward when she can and avoid being snobby when you're on top or angry about life's setbacks when things are not going well.

Above all, love with a sincere heart, operate with a spirit of gratefulness, live well and good while continuing to improve on and building your character and your life. Dr. Renee Dupree believes true greatness shows up when you live to give. This book will change your perspective on life. Get ready for a dramatic change for the better in your life; you have greatness in you.

Les Brown, Motivational Speaker, Author

SUCCESS PRINCIPLE #1

Examine Your Mindset

⌒

If you change the way you look at things, the things you look at change."
–DR. WAYNE DYER

You will soon be able to answer two important questions:

1) What is a mindset?

2) How can my mindset help or hurt me as I rebuild my life?

Let's look first at the <u>definition</u>:

Mindset is an attitude, disposition or mood; an intention or inclination.

- So, the word "mindset" has a lot to do with what you're thinking.

- In this workbook, mindset refers to what you believe about yourself and your ability to experience success in rebuilding your life.

Everyone wants to be a success in their endeavors. So, what keeps some from ever attaining it? In many cases it's simply due to the fact that they overlook the work it takes to truly succeed in life. Success – which includes moving beyond overwhelming setbacks -- doesn't just happen. It is a slow progression of taking one step at a time on a long journey that is sometimes wrought with obstacles. Despite how long it takes, those who ultimately experience success are those who first have a vision and then are persistent in their goals, creating action steps that help them forge forward. Day by day and goal by goal they plough forward until one day they realize they have overcome personal devastation, and success is theirs!

Below are some basic steps toward changing your mindset:

Get Inspired

Inspiration can be a great thing. It is often what moves us forward toward a new goal or dream. More than just motivation, inspiration is the secret key to success.

> *While becoming motivated can excite you, being inspired is the drive to keep going no matter how difficult the journey.*

Inspiration creates action. Let's look at a perfect example of this: *dieting.* You step on the scale or squeeze into last year's bathing suit and suddenly become motivated to lose weight. You join the gym, order some of those diet shakes and get started. You lose a few pounds, but then your motivation wanes. What happens next? In the vast majority of cases, you stop dieting and exercising.

Now, let's look at someone who gets *inspired* to lose weight. They visit their doctor and discover that they have diabetes and heart issues. Their doctor warns that if they don't get serious about losing weight they are going to get sick – very, very sick – and possibly even die. Suddenly, their motivation has changed to inspiration. This person is now inspired to lose weight and get their health back on track. They begin the same way as the last person, instead, after losing a few pounds they find themselves even more inspired to keep going.

Motivation helps people get excited and get started on a project, but it is inspiration that keeps them moving toward their goal.

Finding that kind of inspiration isn't always an easy task. More often than not, the inspiration which sends us off in a new direction is also what makes us squirm, feel uncomfortable, and maybe even a bit hesitant. It can be scary to take steps toward a better self-image, a new dream, and a better life, but this is where success lies.

Find Your Vision

What is it you really want to accomplish? Maybe it's steady, full-time employment. Or, you may want to be able to forgive your husband for betraying you so that you can begin to feel better about yourself again and move forward. Perhaps you want to experience a successful reentry into your community after being incarcerated for several years. Whatever you want to accomplish, without a vision, you will have nothing to drive you.

EXERCISE #1:
YOUR VISION AND YOUR 5 SENSES

Allow yourself about 15 minutes to complete this helpful exercise. Follow these 4 simple steps:

In a place away from distraction, take a few minutes to clarify in your mind **one** thing that you want to accomplish in the process of rebuilding your life.

Close your eyes and create a detailed vision of this accomplishment using **all** of your 5 senses:

What does your accomplishment **look** like: *what colors are you wearing? Are you inside or outside? What color are the walls, or the flowers?*

What does your accomplishment **feel** like: *How do you feel – excited? Proud? Extremely happy? Relaxed?*

What does your accomplishment **sound** like?: *Are you in a quiet place? With a noisy crowd? Are there birds singing and bees humming? Do you hear the sound of children playing? Are people cheering and clapping?*

What does your accomplishment **taste** like? *Your favorite meal or dessert?*

What does your accomplishment **smell** like? *Roses? Your favorite cologne? Popcorn? Barbecue?*

Now, play a "movie" of this accomplishment in your mind: Slowly rerun what it looks, feels, sounds, tastes, and smells like. Experiencing your accomplishment with all of your senses will make it very clear in your mind!

Repeat this exercise daily. Expand it by focusing on other accomplishments you want to envision as you rebuild your life!

Take a Stand

Vision usually begins with a passion for something. Look at Beth Holloway. When her daughter, Natalee, disappeared while on vacation, she took her passion for finding her daughter (who was later pronounced dead) and now helps other families look for lost loved ones. Her passion became a vision for helping others. She was featured her own television series and has a thriving organization that helps loved ones get answers when a child, spouse, friend, or other loved one either disappears or dies under suspicious circumstances.

> *Take a stand on a subject and watch your vision transform itself into action.*

THINK & SHARE

Think about the following questions. Use the space below to jot down your thoughts, then share some of your thoughts with the group.

➢ Have you ever taken a personal stand on any issue in the past. In other words, have you ever <u>not</u> backed down from your intentions in a situation?

➢ How did taking a stand make you **feel**?

➢ What kind of stand could you take that might help you to rebuild your life?

Find the Power Within

There is one ingredient to success that many people overlook: the power within. There are some people who, try as they might, will never succeed. The reason is that they never find a way to tap their own *internal* powers to make their dreams a reality.

Successfully rebuilding your life takes courage, and courage takes power. And it is that power that will define your character and show people who and what you are. It is your internal strength that molds you and makes you the person you are and will make the difference between your success and your failure.

To find the power within, you will want to answer a few questions (be honest!):

1) What are my goals and aspirations?

2) Why do I want to accomplish these things?

3) What am I trying to build for myself? My family? My community?

4) What do I hope to offer the world with the work I do?

5) What truly excites me when it comes to my goals?

> *With the proper mindset and*
> *internal power,*
> *you will be able to find the drive to*
> *continue when roadblocks*
> *get in your way.*

Answering the 5 questions above will help you to better understand where you are going and why, so that you can successfully obtain your life and business goals.

Believe in Yourself

If the power within is so important to success, why do so many people lack it? The answer is simple: they fail to believe in themselves. And that can be detrimental to success. Why? If you don't (or can't) believe in yourself and your ability to succeed, how can anyone else believe in you?

Why would a client trust you to get the job done if you don't believe in your own abilities?

If you lack confidence, then work on building it. Check your posture; stand straight and tall even when you don't feel like it. Learn to speak with authority so that people will listen to you. Act with resolution and people will take notice. Above all else, believe that you can and will succeed.

WORKSHEET

Are You Your Own Worst Enemy? Take This Quiz and Find Out!

It is not uncommon for us to sabotage our own efforts at success without ever realizing that we are even doing it. Are you your own worst enemy? Answer these simple questions to find out:

- Do I often tell myself negative things about my abilities?
- Do I often get close to success, only to experience some unexpected setback?
- Do I procrastinate; especially when it comes to achieving my goals?
- Do I always think someone else deserves success more than I do?

If you answered yes to one or more of these questions, you could possibly be sabotaging your own efforts. Take the time now to learn how to speak kindly to yourself and to begin to believe that you <u>can</u> rebuild your life! Success is yours – all you have to do is take it!

Let's dig a bit deeper into **Success Principle #1: Examine Your Mindset.** Below you will find 4 ways to <u>apply</u> this important principle to your life:

- A group discussion question
- A self-survey
- Some questions for small group discussion
- A role-play scenario

GROUP DISCUSSION QUESTION

Why does it matter what you believe about yourself?

Take a few minutes to jot down your thoughts in the space provided below:

MINDSET SELF-SURVEY #1

This short survey will help you to become more aware of what you believe about yourself, **today, at this moment.** A second Mindset Self-Survey with the same questions appears at the end of this workbook.

Circle the best answer for each statement. (Note: This survey is your personal information; share it with others only if you choose to do so.)

1. The way I was raised as a child is a major reason why I now need to rebuild my life.

Strongly agree Slightly agree Slightly disagree Strongly disagree

Comments(optional):

_____

_____

_____

2. My circumstance (being an addict, betrayed, unemployed, incarcerated, a survivor, or other devastating circumstance) has put a limit on what I can achieve in society.

Strongly agree Slightly agree Slightly disagree Strongly disagree

Comments(optional):

_____

_____

_____

3. My lack of education and skill will hold me back as I rebuild my life.

Strongly agree Slightly agree Slightly disagree Strongly disagree

Comments(optional):

_____

_____

_____

4. In order for me to succeed, I must succeed on my own; no one can really help me.

Strongly agree Slightly agree Slightly disagree Strongly disagree

Comments(optional):

_____

_____

_____

5. I have a great amount of control over my future.

Strongly agree Slightly agree Slightly disagree Strongly disagree

Comments(optional):

_____

_____

_____

6. I know what my passion is.

Strongly agree Slightly agree Slightly disagree Strongly disagree

Comments(optional):

_____

_____

_____

7. I have clear goals for what I want to achieve in the next 5 years.

Strongly agree Slightly agree Slightly disagree Strongly disagree

Comments(optional):

_____

_____

_____

8. A lot of other people deserve success more than I do.

Strongly agree Slightly agree Slightly disagree Strongly disagree

Comments(optional):

_____

_____

_____

9. The present is not as important as the future.

Strongly agree Slightly agree Slightly disagree Strongly disagree

Comments(optional):

_____

_____

_____

10. In order to succeed, I need money more than anything else.

Strongly agree Slightly agree Slightly disagree Strongly disagree

Comments(optional):

_____

_____

_____

Small Group Discussion

In small groups of 3 to 4 people, take about 20 minutes to talk about **mindset.** At the end of your discussion, please share your answers with the whole group.

Below are some questions to discuss.

a. What barriers do you know you will face as you rebuild your life?

b. What kind of mindset is necessary to overcome these barriers?

c. What mindset has held you back or caused problems for you in the past?

d. What's the most important thing you can do to develop a mindset that will help you to experience success putting your life back together?

e. Is there anything that might get in the way of developing a successful mindset?

Use this space to make NOTES to share with the full group:

ROLE PLAY

Note: This role play can be done 2 or 3 different times using different volunteers, depending on class attendance and available time.

Participants:

Volunteer #1 – Bernard, incarcerated out in 113 days

Volunteer #2 – Bernard's Uncle Freddy

Scenario:

- Bernard's been incarcerated for over 6 years (he was the driver in an armed robbery).

- He's decided that with only 113 days left before being released, he needs to get busy preparing for his release date.

- Bernard calls his uncle, the man who has steadily visited and encouraged him for 6 years.

- Bernard expresses doubt and frustration with his chances of finding work.

- Uncle Freddy doesn't sugar-coat the challenges, but he encourages Bernard to keep a positive mindset.

[Those who are not participating in the role play can use the space below to make comments that can be shared with the participants.]

"The biggest game you will ever play is the game in your mind. Master your mind, master your world." -- Kevin Abdulrahman, author

SUCCESS PRINCIPLE #2:

Train Your Mind to Win

❧

"You were born to win, but to be a winner, you must plan to win,

prepare to win, and expect to win."

ZIG ZIGLAR

No one can do the job the way you can! That is a fact. When it comes to doing what needs to be done to overcome a significant devastation – whether it's betrayal by a spouse or the death of a loved one – in order to achieve personal success, you are the only one for the job. Before you can begin to implement any plan, you first have to train your mind to win – i.e., to overcome every obstacle

that gets in the way of rebuilding your life. Until you believe in yourself and your abilities from deep within, your rebuilt life is always going to be just an arm's length away. Of course, believing in yourself is not always easy. That is why you need to learn how to train your mind to win.

Like an athlete who trains his or her body for the event at hand, you can train your mind to take on the challenges you face, and overcome them!

How do you train your mind to think about success? Start by remembering that training is a *process* of getting better. Your thinking won't change immediately, but it will change as long as you *keep training!*

We have broken down this success principle into several "training exercises." These exercises should become part of your daily mental workout. Together, they will reshape your brain so that you will deal more easily with all the challenges that you will run into as you put your life back together.

Exercise #1: Believe in Yourself!

Begin by believing in yourself and your abilities to get the job done. God has equipped you with everything you need. Now you just have to believe that you can do it. In his book "The Obvious," author Bill Walsh reiterates the importance of believing in yourself when he explains simply that "keeping your WHY alive drives your action."

Simply put, if you do not believe <u>why</u> you can do something, then you will not have the drive to move forward toward accomplishing even the smallest step, let alone a dream. **Help give yourself a boost of self-confidence by:**

- writing down all the reasons why you want to accomplish a specific goal
- listing the things that make you unique to accomplishing this task
- explaining to yourself why God has chosen you for this task
- listing all of the things that you are good at (if you can't think of any, ask the people around you for help). Your list might include things like: being friendly, assertive, compassionate, a hard-worker, well-organized, time sensitive, deadline-oriented, and more.

Exercise #2: Keep Your Emotions in Check

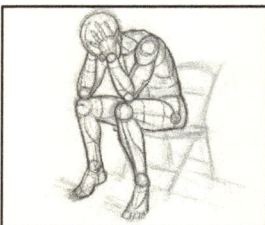

Don't let your emotions tell you what to think or what to do. When we allow our emotional selves to dictate our actions, the result is usually inaction. When you feel your most inept, take a step back and look at where you are headed as well as where you have been. Write down everything you have accomplished with regard to chasing your dream and **list your every accomplishment, no matter how small or seemingly insignificant.**

When you feel your emotions starting to become extreme (depressed, angry, worried), look at this list to remember:

➢ what is <u>true</u> about yourself

➢ what you <u>desire</u> to achieve

➢ that you are <u>capable</u> of achieving your desire

THINK & SHARE

▪ Do you think that writing down your accomplishments and reviewing them as suggested above will help you to keep your emotions in check?

▪ Jot down your <u>honest</u> thoughts below and share with others:

Exercise #3: Develop Internal Strength

As you work on your external goals, it is also important to work on your internal strengths. There will be many challenges along your specific path toward a new life, and being ready to face those challenges will require a certain amount of internal strength and fortitude. If you don't know how to build your internal strength, find someone you admire and trust who you know is strong on the inside, and just talk to them about what makes them strong. You can also read some books or attend some seminars on the subject. If you still need support in this area, don't hesitate to see a counselor who is trained at helping people work on their internal views and character.

Exercise #4: Discipline Yourself

Training your mind to win requires a certain amount of discipline. You have to be disciplined enough to be able to get to work on a task and keep at it until it is completed. Once your mind sees you plugging along (and succeeding) it will be much easier to believe that you can indeed accomplish anything!

Discipline allows your mind to grasp the fact that you are more than capable of great things.

Here's a 2-part tip on staying disciplined:

- Keep photos of the person, people, or dream that motivates you. You can also find a magazine or internet picture of your dream – for instance, if you've always wanted to be a chef, find a photo of someone wearing a chef's hat, or of a gourmet kitchen!

- Post those photos of your loved ones and your dreams in places where they're never far from your sight!

Exercise #5: Develop Personal Character

Personal character – your values and principles that define you as a person -- will be the foundation of your success. Without it, you will undermine your own efforts and end up failing at the task ahead. Take the time to build your personal character in order to know what decisions to make when it becomes harder and harder to distinguish between the right ones and the wrong ones. And when you seem to be veering off track, tempted to take a short cut and compromise your principles, remember this important message from I Corinthians 10:13:

"No temptation has overtaken you that is not common to man. God is faithful, and he will not let you be tempted beyond your ability, but with the temptation he will also provide the way of escape, that you may be able to endure it."

You can develop personal character by honoring your principles – the things you value so much that you aren't willing to compromise on them, things like:

- Being a person of your word

- Working hard

- Putting family first

- Always putting forth your best effort

GROUP DISCUSSION

Jasmine completed an addiction recovery program 4 months ago. She has found a decent job working as a receptionist for a nonprofit organization.

- As part of her job, Jasmine orders office supplies.

- Jasmine really needs to learn a software program called Photoshop so that she can apply for higher-paying jobs.

- Jasmine knows for sure that if she orders the Photoshop program through her job and takes it home to learn on her own, no one would notice.

- Jasmine works full-time and has two kids at home. She can't think of any other way to learn Photoshop.

If you were Jasmine:

- What would you do?

- What might be the outcome of your decision?

Exercise #6: Learn to Focus

When you focus on your project (or dream), you are training your mind to build resolve, overcome challenges and achieve success. While focusing on your dream is important, *how* you focus is equally important.

How deeply you focus on your goals and dreams will determine whether or not you succeed in accomplishing them. The biggest mistake most people make is focusing on the big picture instead of a small part of the picture. Rather than focusing all of your attention on the ultimate goal, try instead to zone in on one small aspect of your dream.

Choose one goal or one action step that can get you closer to fulfillment. That way you can concentrate on a manageable piece of the greater puzzle. Once you have successfully fit that piece into place, move on to the next one, and the next, and so forth.

Avoid distractions and procrastination as much as possible. Before long, you will realize that this type of precision focus results in a job well done. **Here are 3 tips to avoid distractions:**

- Decide each day on <u>one</u> thing that you want to accomplish.

- Focus your positive energy on accomplishing that one thing.

- If you find yourself getting off track, pay attention to what got you off track so that you can address it head-on or avoid it altogether in the future.

Focusing your mind is not always easy, but it is well worth the effort. If this is an unusual way of thinking for you, then take the time to integrate some of the tips above to help wrap your mind around the fact that you are poised for success.

Discussion Questions:

- ➢ *What is one major distraction that you have to deal with every day, right now?*

- ➢ *How can you focus so that the distraction does not keep you from making progress toward rebuilding your life?*

Exercise #7: Break Negative Patterns

Lack of self-confidence may be one of the biggest culprits to killing people's dreams and keeping them from succeeding. Finding your internal power requires a certain amount of self-confidence and faith in your own abilities, and if you lack that, failure is inevitable. After all, if you don't believe in yourself, why should anyone else? No one wakes up in the morning with the attitude that today is the day you are going to sabotage your own efforts for success. Yet, we all do that exact thing – every day!

Let me explain. We all have an internal dialogue that tells us what we think we can – and cannot – accomplish. For some of us this internal conversation focuses on what you don't want, rather than on what you want --which can be a real dream killer!

Here is an example. Let's say you find out about a new job opportunity at work. It's a big leap from your current position. Still, those around you keep telling you to apply. Your brain says yes, but your internal conversation says no. Take a moment to listen to the voice in your head. Is it saying things like, "Oh, I'm not qualified for that job," or "It's so different from what I do now I would be lost..." ? If so, then you are falling victim to negative speak.

Now, try and change that dialogue to things like, "That job needs a real organizer and I'm great at that," or you might say, "Sure, there are things I won't know if I get that job, but I'll talk with others in the office, take a night class or seek other help if it means getting a job I'll love."

See the difference? One set of thoughts tells you all of the reasons why you aren't good enough for that job while the other helps you see what you can offer and ways in which you can beat any deficits in experience.

We do not need other people to discourage us. We as humans are great at doing it to ourselves. But there is good news! Now that you know what you are doing, you can *change* the way you talk to yourself. You hold the key to your success. You know how great you are – now believe it. Stand up to your internal doubts and stamp them out. How? Here are a few tricks:

Become aware of your thoughts

Allowing negative chatter to eat away at your self-confidence and motivation is a sure-fire way to fail. Still, we all tend to do it anyway.

Today is the day to get out of your own way and change those inner doubts into positive comments!

Stop beating yourself up over something you think you lack or did wrong. Instead, become your own cheerleader, acknowledging the wonderful things you are (and do), and congratulating yourself every time you accomplish a task – even a small one.

This isn't going to be easy. Most of us shy away from patting ourselves on the back. Maybe it's because it seems self-absorbed and egotistical. But, if we don't tell ourselves how awesome we are (at least in our heads), then we are going to show ourselves as a person who is less than capable to the outside world.

Take a look at yourself in the mirror. Do you exude confidence and ability? If not, then you have to start being nicer to yourself. Once you acknowledge how detrimental those negative self-talks are and realize how often you scold yourself internally, you can begin to change the conversation. As soon as you recognize that negative chatter, alter it to the exact opposite.

Let's say that you miss an important phone call with a client. Instead of scolding yourself and telling yourself how irresponsible you are, tell yourself something like, "Okay, I missed the call because I was busy doing something else that is important. It's not the end of the world. I can fix this. I will call the client and explain what happened and apologize. I will do whatever it takes to make this right." This type of conversation will give you a more authoritative tone when speaking with the client and will make them perceive you more as a busy businessperson who had to handle an emergency rather than an unreliable one. Maybe they will forgive you and maybe they won't. Either way, giving yourself negative chatter is not going to help the situation and could even make it worse.

Turn every negative into a positive

It's a real shame how we sabotage ourselves so easily. Someone may tell us something, and while it may hurt our feelings or even anger us, we can often step away from the conversation with our ego and confidence still intact. Not so with our own internal thoughts. Those negative thoughts we tell ourselves can often do more damage than the worst slighting by another. So, what can we do to change our internal dialogue and give ourselves the right message?

Have you ever heard the saying "Turn that frown upside down"? Well, you can do the same with your internal chatter. It is possible to turn those negative comments into positive ones. One way is to be cognizant of what you are telling yourself and take any negative comment and twist it into a positive one. Another is to simply feed yourself positive chatter. While you will have to concentrate to do this at first, after a little practice it should simply become second nature.

One strategy that some people prefer is to physically "turn off" the negative chatter by tapping their forehead slightly in a manner that reminds them that the off button has been pushed. This is a physical way for their brain to acknowledge those negative thoughts and tune them out.

We all know people who are just naturally pleasant, happy and full of confidence. Most of us look at these souls and wonder how in the world they can be so content with themselves. The reason is because they have made a conscious decision to only tell themselves positive things. That simple change allows them to be the person they want to be. When their own brain stops sabotaging their efforts, they are able to go after their dreams more fearlessly. So can you.

Turn off that negative chatter and replace it with healthier, happier, and more contented talk! You are your own best advocate and cheerleader — so start cheering!

Let's practice! Below is a list of "useless words," followed by an exercise on what to say, along with some discussion questions.

Useless Words to Avoid

There are some words that simply strip us of self-confidence and keep us from success. What are these dangerous words? Here are just a few:

TRY The word "try" implies failure. Instead, replace it with "DO." Stop trying and start doing.

CAN'T The next useless word to toss from your vocabulary is the word "can't." It has only two possibilities: you either don't know how to do something, or you don't want to do something; both of which can be remedied.

BUT The last useless word to avoid is the word "but." It is just an excuse.

The scary thing about these insidious words is how they change the way you act and react to yourself and your business.

Get rid of the above words right now and replace them with some of these words instead:

KNOW Knowing is the act of confidence and the security of being sure in your ability.

WHEN The word "when" makes things happen. It requires commitment to answer a "when" question.

CHALLENGES There are no problems in business – just challenges. Simply making this change can help you tell yourself that what you are facing can be handled – and fixed. Problems are hard to fix, but not challenges – they are made to be overcome.

It may seem overly simplistic to change a few words in your vocabulary and expect big change. But, remember, small changes can -- and will -- have a big impact on how you handle yourself and your daily progress!

More Ways to Speak Differently

This basic exercise will help you to more positively see what's possible for you!

Instead of	Say this
I can't or I'll try	I want to . . .
	I need to . . .
	I'm pretty sure I can . . .
	Give me some time to think about . . .
	I'll do whatever I need to do to . . .
	I'm not going to do that because . . .

Discussion Questions:

- What are some other ways that people talk negatively about themselves?

- How would you flip these negative comments to make them positive?

SUCCESS PRINCIPLE #3

Have the Strength and the Courage to Fight for Your Dreams

❧

"A dream doesn't become a reality through magic; it takes sweat, determination, and hard work."

COLIN POWELL

Rebuilding your life takes courage. It isn't always easy (or fun) to stand on that ledge and take a leap into the unknown. But for those who can find the strength and courage to fight for their dreams, success is inevitable.

Right now, you may be at a point where you've begun making some real success toward putting your life back together, but you're feeling weary, doubtful, and intimidated by the idea of failure – don't! This is the point where the vast majority of people walk away, never really giving their dream the time and attention it deserves. What a shame. One more step may have been all that was necessary to experience the success they were after -- and deserved. Yet, without the strength to carry on and the courage to walk into an unknown world, they gave up on themselves and their dream. Don't be one of those people. Instead, gather up the courage and strength to keep moving. Even if it means using the smallest steps possible.

Even a small step is better than no step at all.

Stop Listening to Naysayers

I've said it before, but I am going to say it again: surround yourself with encouraging people. And if you can't, then keep your plans to yourself.

> *Nothing will sap your courage and strength faster than someone you trust telling you over and over again that you cannot accomplish what you set out to do.*

Whether they are doing it on purpose or not doesn't really matter. What matters is the effect their words have on your actions. Success Principle #4 will take a closer look at naysayers – who we call "dream stealers."

Make a commitment

It has been said that it takes a long time to grow an old friend. The same can be said for working toward your new life. Success with your personal growth -- which includes feeling good about who you are, presenting yourself to others with self-confidence, and achieving your career or life goals – does not happen overnight. It takes months or even years for slow-moving progress to become a reality. So, what does that mean for you? It means that:

If you are not prepared to commit to a long period of time to build your strengths and build your future, then success will remain ELUSIVE.*
*Difficult to find

That means that you have to show up every day with an attitude that you will succeed, even when the road is rough. And it means chipping away at your goals one small step or project at a time. If it's solid employment that you need, be willing to put in the long hours and take on the lousy jobs in order to prove yourself worthy in the business world and build a reputation that is long-lasting.

COMMITMENT + DAILY EFFORT + TIME = A RENEWED SELF + NEW OPPORTUNITIES

Sure, some people will seem to come out of nowhere and experience great success overnight. But, take a closer look. Did they really? What may appear to be instant success to the outside world may in reality have taken years of behind-the-scenes work that no one ever noticed until one day – bam! That person's efforts got noticed and they seemed to spiral into the spotlight.

It has been documented in the business world that it takes 10,000 hours of work before a product is ready for mass market. Are you ready to put 10,000 hours (that's 40 hours a week for 5 years) into your project before you expect it to even be ready for unveiling? Most of us simply aren't.

In a world where fast food, quick responses and overnight delivery are the norm, it can be difficult for the average person to even comprehend how much time and energy goes into rebuilding yourself, or creating a successful business – or even a single product or service. Now is a good time to begin wrapping your mind (and attitude) around this fact. If you are not ready to stick it out for the long haul, you may want to reconsider your goals and begin again when you are ready to accept the fact that great success will come when you fully commit yourself to success.

Which leads us to our next point . . . the importance of getting started

Don't Just Dream – Get Moving!

Which leads us to our next point . . . the importance of getting started or even cures for deadly disease lay in dust beneath those tombstones. Why? Because the people with the ideas never got off their duffs and did anything about it. Don't be one of them! Get moving – right now! **(Keep reading in this section and you will find several exercises to help you better understand what a "dream" is, and how you can actively go after yours!)**

No one can make you a success; only you can do it. Even if God wants you to be a new person and has given you the gifts you need to accomplish your vision, it will not happen if you never **do** anything to accomplish it.

Going after your dreams is hard work. It takes time . . . it takes commitment . . . it takes perseverance . . . is takes fortitude and most of all, it takes **work:** your determination and consistent effort to learn from your past, to allow your pain to receive healing counsel, and to move confidently into a fulfilling life experience. Know that you can find within yourself the strength to do what is required to achieve your goals!

Let's take a closer look at what your dreams are. The examples and exercises below will also help you to know WHAT and WHO you are fighting in order to keep your dreams alive.

Discussion Question:

What is a dream?

FIRST, think about your answer, jot some notes below, then discuss.

Below are 4 activities based on 4 simple truths about your dream:

1. Your dreams are priceless.
2. Your dreams are something to protect.
3. Your dreams are worth fighting for.
4. Your dreams can remain dreams, or with your hard work, they can become your reality.

1. ROLE PLAY - Your dreams are priceless

Volunteer #1 – Sheila, a recovering addict

Volunteer #2 – Gail, Sheila's friend

Scenario:

- Sheila is in a 12-step program for gamblers.
- She loves art and her dream is to be healthy enough to travel to Europe to visit world-famous art galleries.
- Sheila believes the following about her dream:
- Her dream gives her something to live for.
- Her dream kept her together when she lost everything else.
- Without her dream she knows that she can have everything and still feel completely empty.
- Her dream is priceless.
- Gail doesn't understand why Sheila's dream is so important.
- Sheila tries to explain to Gail how important her dream is.

2. SMALL GROUP DISCUSSION - Your dreams are something to protect

Don't cast your pearls before swine, lest they be trampled! (from Matthew 7:6)

Form groups of 3-4 people and spend 15 minutes discussing the following question:

What does it mean to cast your pearls before swine?

Use the space below to jot down notes. At the end of your discussion, share your thoughts with the entire group.

3. THINK & SHARE – Your dreams are worth fighting for

Think about and list below at least 3 ways that you can fight for your dreams *without using violence*. Share your responses with the group.

4. Your dreams can remain dreams, or with hard work, they can become your REALITY

➤ You have help! If you are spiritual, you have Divine guidance. There are also people, videos, and books you can rely on to help you begin setting life-rebuilding goals for yourself that make sense.

➤ You have a full "mental exercise" program (see SUCCESS PRINCIPLE TWO) that you can rely on to develop a positive mental attitude and build your inner strength.

➤ You have a strong motivation (family, friends, and/or other things) that keep you focused on making your dreams real.

GROUP DISCUSSION – GETTING KNOCKED DOWN

As you begin working toward your dreams, you <u>will</u> experience frustrations, setbacks, and failures! All successful people have failed many times – but they used their failures to motivate them toward their future success.

How do <u>you</u> do this?

- ❖ **See** your failure as a learning opportunity.
- ❖ **Use** your failure to motivate you to get better.
- ❖ **Silence** your failure by not allowing it to dominate your thoughts or discourage your future action.

You can always respond to setbacks and failures in a way that moves you forward!

Write your thoughts on the above statement in the space below.

SUCCESS PRINCIPLE #4

Learn to Identify Dream Stealers

❧

"Don't let someone who gave up on their dreams talk you out of yours."

Identifying

DREAM STEALERS

Everyone has them in their life: people who tend to discourage those around them. No matter how great the idea or accomplishment, they seem to find something wrong with it – or with you. Maybe it is a critical mother; a depressed friend; or a hard-to-please spouse. This type of person is called a dream stealer and if you aren't careful, they will strip away your confidence and keep you from going after success.

⚠️

I have known more than my share of dream stealers in my life. Here are just a few examples of how some dream stealers kept the people in their lives from going after the success they deserved.

One friend told me the story of her mother, who had absolutely no confidence in herself and allowed that lack of confidence to be pushed onto her children. At a very young age, my friend wanted to go to college to become a journalist. Coming from a very poor family in a small factory town, this was a very lofty (and unheard of) dream. Instead of encouraging her daughter to do well in school and apply for scholarships, this mother would say things like, "No one from this town ever goes to college," and, "A child of mine isn't smart enough to become something like that" or, "Have you ever heard of anyone from around here becoming a journalist?" Eventually my friend was beaten down by these remarks and put her dream on hold, until one day she met someone that she shared her secret desire with and he said, "Wow, that's really interesting. So what are you going to do to make it happen?" Suddenly, she found herself inspired to accomplish her goal and you know what? She worked as a journalist for more than 20 years!

Here is another example of a more subtle dream stealer. When Matt told a friend that he was applying for a promotion at work, his friend (who Matt later learned had applied for a similar job and was turned down), said things like:

- "You're not going to like that job"
- "That job is going to be really hard for you"
- "Aren't there more qualified people applying?"
- "Won't a job like that take you away from your family?"

Although he wasn't blatantly negative, the subtlety of his remarks began to eat away at Matt's confidence and he began to doubt himself. Luckily, he had others at work and home who encouraged him to apply, and within weeks he was promoted to a new position that he found both rewarding and successful.

As you can see from the examples above, ***dream stealers are naysayers who always have something negative to say.*** Instead of offering concrete tips and ideas on how the person can overcome adversity, they spend their time always pointing out all of the negatives (both real and perceived), and never offering any kind of real encouragement.

Discussion Question:

Why do you need to protect yourself against dream stealers?

<u>Use the space below to jot down NOTES.</u>

Who Is a Dream Stealer?

Dream stealers are a dime a dozen. We all know more than a few. They can be: your spouse; your best friend; even the sweet grandmother type living next door. Why, I even knew a pastor once who was a major dream stealing culprit. The sad thing is that most of these people don't even realize that they are dream stealers, which makes their comments even more dangerous. When you come across a deliberate dream stealer, you can thwart their attempts at driving you away from your dreams. But, when those comments come from someone you would never expect to want to discourage you, they can be harder to push aside – or push through.

<u>BECOMING AWARE</u>

Psychologists have discovered four main types of dream stealers. Following each description below, there's room for you to write in the name of one person you know who fits that description.

1. The Unintentional Dream Stealer

This type of dream stealer really has no idea what they are doing and in most cases, they mean absolutely no harm by their comments. **They simply offer their opinions (over and over again), which tend to be more negative than positive.** There is good news when dealing with an unintentional dream stealer. Since they mean no harm, they can often be persuaded to see how their comments are actually not helpful. Keep in mind to do this very kindly and delicately as to not make them react defensively to what you are saying.

- Do you know anyone like this?

_____

2. The Concerned Dream Stealer

While not as obvious about their comments as the unintentional dream stealer, the concerned dream stealer may have an inkling of what they are doing, but are doing it out of concern. **This type of person loves you so much that they cannot bear to see you hurt, so they try to dissuade you from taking any chances.** Their goal is not to strip away your dreams, but to protect you, ensuring that you live a nice, safe and secure life, devoid of disappointment.

- And who's one person you know like this?

_____

3. Intentional Dream Stealer

Now we come to a more insidious type of dream stealer: the person who knows exactly what they are doing, yet does it anyway. **This is the person who can't stand to see someone else succeed, so they ago out of their way to discourage them.** Sometimes they are subtle and sometimes their attempts are more blatant. The intentional dream stealer is usually the person with little confidence. They don't know how to go after their own dreams, so they decide that they cannot allow others to go after theirs, lest they feel less important in life.

- Does a name come to mind?

_____

4. The Jealous Dream Stealer

Maybe the most dangerous of all dream stealers, **the jealous dream stealer often works behind the scenes to ensure that you miss out on opportunities or that you fail to act when an opportunity does arise.** Unable to fulfill their own dreams, they simply abhor the fact that anyone else may achieve theirs. They make it their life's ambition to stop you from accomplishing your dream. These are silent saboteurs who can be very cunning and very subtle when it comes to stripping away your confidence or keeping you from success.

- Do you know a jealous type?

See the dream stealers in your life as <u>pathetic</u> rather than powerful!

Ways to Keep Your Dreams Safe

Now that you know what type of dream stealers to watch out for, the odds are good that you will begin to notice more than a few in your life. Since you can now recognize their motives, you may be wondering how to thwart their efforts. Here are a few basic tips on ways to keep your dreams safe and continue on your journey toward success:

Keep Quiet

When a new opportunity comes your way, you may be tempted to shout it from the rooftops – don't! Most dreams get stolen when we share too much (especially with family). In big business, people often worry that their client, or product or idea will "get stolen" by a competitor, when in reality their success may be in greater danger from their friends and family. Maybe Uncle Mel isn't going to steal your idea and sell it on the open market, but he just might steal your confidence and thwart your dream, keeping you from becoming a success. So, what's the

lesson here? Share as little as you can. Your dreams can't get stolen if you keep them to yourself!

Share Your Successes (and leave your failures behind)

Sharing your successes can help you (and everyone around you) see the validity in your dream, and give you more credibility. Plus, sharing a success with a dream stealer takes away their power. Now, share your failures too and you are setting yourself up for more negative attention —and remarks. Let everyone know when you succeed, and keep those failures to yourself!

Know How to Fight Back

You have decided to share your dream with only a few select people in your life and then it happens – someone lets your plans slip to a dream stealer. Oops! Now that person is gunning for you, ready to let you know exactly why you cannot succeed with your plans. If you don't expect it, their negative attacks may indeed stop you in your tracks. But, if you think about how to respond to negative dream stealing attention before it is thrust upon you, you will have a much better chance of surviving the blast.

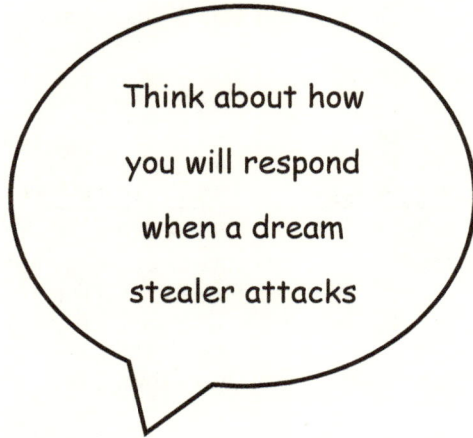

Having a few good comeback lines, or ways to evade their questions and change the subject in your arsenal, can help you to avoid the fallout should it come your way.

One way to do this is to  write down the names of **all** of the people in your life that you may consider a dream stealer. Then write down things they might possibly say to steer you away from your dream. Finally, write down a way that you can counteract their attack in a loving and kind manner. There is no need to be rude, disrespectful or mean when dealing with these people. But, you must be firm in your knowledge that you are on the right track and are following a winning plan for your life and business.

Remember, your dreams belong to you! During those times when you feel like the people around you are trying to tear down your fortitude and get you to change course, pray for patience, understanding and perseverance. The dream stealers in your life may be out to keep you from attaining the kind of success you are after, but that does not mean they will succeed. Stay the course no matter what they say or do to thwart your efforts.

Next, let's practice with a role play.

Role Play – Keeping Your Dream Safe

Volunteer #1: Dante, the dreamer

Volunteer #2: Jay, the dream stealer

Scenario:

- Dante lost his daughter in a car accident.
- Dante sees the world differently now, and wants to go to school to become a social worker.
- Dante shares his dream with Jay, his best friend.
- Jay tries to steal his dream.

This role play can be done with different volunteers playing the roles; volunteers can feel free to choose different dreams if they want.

When all the role plays are complete, discuss them as a group.

"People who say it cannot be done should not interrupt those who are doing it."

SUCCESS PRINCIPLE #5

Have Heart

⁓

*"It's part of life to have obstacles. It's about **overcoming** obstacles — that's the key to happiness."*

Herbie Hancock

Have heart! When the road gets hard and you are left weary by the side of the road toward success, you are not alone. Sometimes the road to success is wrought with obstacles,et and some of those obstacles may seem more like brick walls that cannot be scaled rather than a basic bump that can be ploughed through. Be wary of allowing yourself to get stuck complaining about the obstacle; find a detour around it!

Have heart: there is always a way around an obstacle. Here are a few questions to ask yourself when you face a problem that seems insurmountable:

1. **What is the problem I'm facing?** Oftentimes we think one thing is the problem when it really is something else. Be sure to look closely at your issue and try and figure out what is causing it.

2. **What can I do to rectify the situation?** Maybe you are finding it difficult to move to the next level at your job or to land that special client. Think of unique ways that may help you to overcome this particular challenge. Think outside of the box here.

3. **What small steps can give me momentum?** Stop trying to solve all of your problems with one big push. Instead, think of one or two small steps that can help move you forward toward your goal.

4. **What can I learn from this experience?** We often face challenges in life and business when we need to learn something. List all of the positives you can take away from this experience. Not only will it help you to avoid the same problems in the future, but it will help make this roadblock seem more bearable.

Once you have answered these simple questions, you may be able to see a clearer path around your problem. At the very least, you should have a clearer idea of what the problem is, and having this awareness can make your counter attack more productive!

SMALL GROUP DISCUSSION

In groups of 3-4 people, **talk about an obstacle you have faced in your life.** Spend about 20 minutes sharing:

> ➤ Were you able to overcome the obstacle?
>
> ➤ How did you overcome it?
>
> ➤ What did you learn from dealing with that obstacle?

LARGE GROUP DISCUSSION

What are some definite obstacles will you face as you rebuild your life?

What will you do to overcome these obstacles?

Discuss this quote:

"There are plenty of difficult obstacles in your path. Don't allow yourself to become one of them."- – Ralph Marston

SUCCESS PRINCIPLE #6:

Say No to Fear

∽

"My fear was not of death itself, but a death without meaning."

HUEY P. NEWTON

One of the biggest obstacles we all face when it comes to striving for success is fear. Yes, it can be extremely frightening to reach beyond your own capabilities and strive to accomplish what looks to be insurmountable. Yet, if you can move past those fears, you can – and will – accomplish everything you set out to do.

Fear is what drives some people toward success – and others to halt before taking the next step. Why? For some, the fear is of the actual work involved in achieving their dreams. Maybe they fear not being good enough or capable of great things. While for others, the fear is of attaining the success itself.

So, what is the driving force behind your own fears?

Is It the Fear of Success?

Not as uncommon as you might first think, the fear of success is often what keeps the majorly of us from even attempting our dreams, let alone doing what is necessary to achieve them.

Feel the fear and do it anyway!

What is there to fear about success? It is different for every person, but here are just some of the reasons why the mere thought of achieving success may be paralyzing you:

- a fear of standing out

- a fear of attention

- a fear of completing the steps necessary to achieve success

- a fear of your life changing in a dramatic manner

Is It a Fear of Leading?

By definition, successful people are leaders. With leadership comes responsibility and many people are afraid to be the one people turn to and count on.

Is It a Fear of Power?

Without a certain amount of power, you will be unable to thrust forward with making significant life changes. Yet, some people shy away from the exact kind of power that will help them to achieve their dreams. If you find yourself shying away from situations that put you in the power seat, be sure to take stock of why you may feel this way and work towards remedying it. Otherwise, you may find yourself always a step or two behind, unable to fulfill your dreams.

Is It a Fear of Encroachment?

Will success take you into unknown territory where you may be the minority? Maybe you are a woman trying to break into a man's world, or some other situation where the people around you may not consider you their equal. Breaking new ground takes a certain amount of confidence that you will need to build before you can move forward in realizing your dream.

Is It a Fear of Inadequacy?

Has your subconscious mind made you feel less than adequate to do the job? This mindset can – and will – keep you from succeeding. Don't fall victim to this lie!

> *Master your skills to help BOOST your confidence and allow yourself to understand how qualified you really are to overcome any challenge standing in your way!*

Is It a Fear of Lost Integrity?

If you are a felon or a recovering addict trying to make it in a judgmental society, you may worry that you will have to make compromises or excuses in order "to make it." That simply is not true.

Yes, the world would have you believe that it is impossible for a person with your background to make it, but nothing is further from the truth. The best way to overcome this concern is to own your past and know you can move forward. Outline your own boundaries before making important decisions. Know exactly what you believe in and what you think is right – and what you know is wrong. Draw that line for yourself so that you know exactly when you are coming close to crossing it. Trouble usually ensues when people don't think about how far they will go to fulfill their dreams, and they make poor choices because of this lack of planning.

Is It a Fear of Failure?

Failure can be a hard thing to handle. Sometimes the fear of it is enough to stop us in our tracks. If you find yourself so worried about failing that you don't even try new things, then you may want to consider that the fear of failure is actually keeping you from even trying to succeed.

HOW SHOULD I RESPOND WHEN I'M AFRAID?

Keep in mind that a certain amount of fear is *normal* when stepping out and trying something new. Sometimes it is even fear that can propel you forward as you use it to energize and invigorate your action plan. Unfortunately, for some people, those fears are more a detriment to their success than an advantage. It is when those fears keep you from moving forward that they become a problem. So, how should you respond when you are afraid? IN FAITH, of course!

And speaking of fear . . .

Many people don't like talking about fear because it's often hard to admit that we experience it. For some, admitting fear means admitting weakness.

But fear doesn't make you weak, it makes you stand still, question your dreams, and doubt your capabilities. **Don't allow fear to bring you down!**

SMALL GROUP DISCUSSION

When you are on your life-rebuilding pathway, you will need to face and overcome your fears. Below are some fears that people who are working to get their lives back on track may experience.

In groups of 3-4 people, discuss **what kind of thinking or action will help you to overcome each type of fear.**

Return to the larger group to share your ideas of **how to overcome** these fears.

- Fear of failure

- Fear of success

- Fear that you are unprepared or not good enough

- Fear of being in a totally new environment

- Fear of being unfairly judged or treated

THINK & SHARE

Choose one of the following quotes. Take a few minutes to think about the full meaning of the quote. Jot down notes below, if you want. Share your thoughts with the larger group:

"Feel the fear and do it anyway." – Tamara Melton

"Courage is knowing what not to fear." – Plato

"We must travel in the direction of our fear." – John Berryman

"True success is overcoming the fear of being unsuccessful." – Paul Sweeney

<u>NOTES</u>

SUCCESS PRINCIPLE #7

Change Your Environment

⌒

If your environment is not to your liking, change it. – Napoleon Hill

Your immediate environment doesn't just consist of the air, trees and water. Your environment includes: people and their opinions; the institutions you visit often (your job, church, the library, the mall, etc.); and the media (news, celebrity hype, and advertising). Your environment has a definite influence on your thinking – that is, what you think about yourself and your ability to successfully navigate through all that's necessary in order to rebuild yourself.

We'll examine this success principle – change your environment -- by taking a closer look at the various elements in your environment, what your environment is telling you, what kind of environment you need in order to make significant changes in your life, and how to go about creating an environment that will support your personal growth.

THE ELEMENTS OF YOUR ENVIRONMENT

Your Family

For many people, the greatest influence in their environment is family – those people who raise us from infancy to at least young adulthood. Your family may be your parents, siblings, grandparents and/or other members of your birth family. Or, your family may be others who raised you, such as friends of your immediate family, foster or adoptive parents, or staff members of institutions, such as hospitals.

Based upon **how** they treat you, such as giving you loving yet firm correction, or constant criticism and punishment – and **what** they tell you about critical matters, such as your honesty, your education, your inner happiness – your family passes on to you a set of values. These values are the things that guide you through all of the circumstances of your life. If your family showed you by their example that you are not very smart and thus education beyond high school is a waste of your time, then you most likely will not value education very highly. The opposite is of course true. How much you value education – and other things, like telling the truth, being on time, and finishing what you start – will greatly influence the choices you make and how you deal with difficult circumstances.

? **Think about: Who in your family do you believe had the greatest influence on your thinking and behavior?**

Your Personal Associations

Who are the people you spend your personal time with outside of work? These are your friends and associates (casual acquaintances). These folks may have some values that are different than yours, but you most likely share some basic values in common, or else you wouldn't spend much time with these people.

Your friends and associates can definitely influence the decisions you make, and because you spend time with these people, you will at least listen to what they have to say and consider it.

Your Job

If you go into an office every day, you are surrounded by co-workers who may not be friends or close associates. You may frequently interact with computers and other technology. You also most likely work in an environment that has some mission statement, as well as an office "culture." If you work from home, you will deal with your workspace and possibly others who may also be in the home. All of these things combine to create your work environment.

You spend many hours at work, so your work environment influences you primarily because of the amount of time you spend there! Whether positive, negative, or neutral, the work you do daily and the environment you do it in will impact your personal growth.

Think about: Do you truly enjoy your job? Why or why not? What do you like or dislike about your work environment?

The Places You Frequent

Where do you spend most of your time outside of work? These are places you may go for entertainment, spiritual encouragement, education, or something else. Each of your "hangouts" has a purpose, and so it's good for you to be aware of the purpose each of your favorite spots holds in your life.

The Media

It's certainly an understatement to say that the media influences your life. Your primary source for news, movies, music, and product information comes through your phone, computer, television, radio, newspaper or magazine. consume on a daily basis about yourself and the

The media that you often tells you how to think world around you.

WHAT IS YOUR ENVIRONMENT TELLING YOU?

Now that you have a good idea of what your environment consists of, be aware that all of the elements that make up your environment are giving you messages about yourself and your ability to succeed in rebuilding your life.

The various exercises below will help you to identify what **messages — i.e., what you see and/or hear** -- from each element of your environment, and whether these messages support or hinder your progress.

Small Group Discussion:
Remembering Family

Values are the beliefs you hold deeply about what's important or what's not important. In groups of 3 to 4, spend about 15 minutes discussing the following:

- What are some of the values that your family passed on to you, not just by what they said, but by what they *did*.

- Do you think that the values you learned from your family have had a mostly positive or negative influence in your life?

When you return to the larger group, be prepared to share any of this discussion that you feel comfortable sharing.

Take just a few minutes to think on your own about the question below. If you like, share your thoughts with the entire group:

The people you choose to spend time with (friends and associates) are often a different group than your co-workers.

> *In your experience, which group has had a more positive influence in your life? Give some examples of why this is true.*

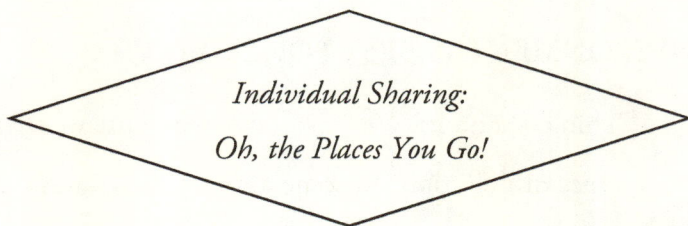

Individual Sharing:
Oh, the Places You Go!

- Each person in the entire group will take a few minutes to think about one place where they have spent time that is mostly negative, and one place where they have spent time that is mostly positive.

- A few volunteers (2 or 3) will share what were some of the negative and positive messages they have received in each of these places.

Large Group Discussion:
Media Matters

➤ What kind of media appeals to you most (such as news, music, sports, celebrity gossip, movies)?

➤ What are some of the messages you receive from your favorite media?

➤ Do these message support or slow your progress toward rebuilding your life?

WHAT ENVIRONMENT IS <u>BEST</u> FOR YOU?

Think about it: We have laws that outlaw certain types of pollution. In some areas of the country and world, there are days when there are "smog alerts." We definitely need air, but not all types of air are breathable! This is also true of your *personal* environment: You need people and institutions in your life, but not every person, group, or institution will support your personal growth.

You know what your environment consists of, and you have a good idea of the kinds of messages you receive from each part of your environment. So, let's now look at what kind of environment is best for you – i.e., what kind of environment do you need in order to make significant changes in your life?

People Who Support You

You will have a most difficult time if you try to rebuild your life completely on your own, without the support of others. You need various kinds of support from people, such as encouragement and even physical help (like transportation and babysitting!). What you need most in people is their belief that you can achieve what you set out to achieve. We'll look further at how to identify these kinds of people later in this section.

Institutions Committed to Your Growth

Everyone would agree that some institutions exist to help you to grow. Schools and online educational programs help you to become more intelligent and skilled, gyms provide training equipment and staff to help you stay fit, recovery programs offer counseling and support groups to help people overcome addiction, and churches are here to advance your spiritual connection and growth. Your best environment for rebuilding your life will include one or more of these kinds of institutions that have your best interests at heart!

Your employer is a type of institution, even if you work for a nonprofit organization or a very small company. Most every company and organization have a clear mission statement that states why they exist. Just as with the various institutions mentioned above, your personal environment should include a workplace that in some way advances your personal goals.

Media that Empowers You

We all like to be entertained. Entertainment is a way to relax our minds after a long or challenging day. But keep in mind that your growth happens through action – i.e., you taking purposeful steps toward your goals and vision. The media in your environment will support your personal growth when it challenges your brain to consider new ideas and points you to the success stories of others.

HOW DO YOU CHANGE YOUR ENVIRONMENT?

What if you realize that your current environment is just not working toward your benefit? You may have an unsupportive family, few real friends, and negative co-workers. Maybe you have a few good friends, but you're not connected with any positive institutions that will help you to grow in your skill set. And maybe at the end of a day, the media you pay closest attention to is not particularly uplifting.

Below are some practical things you can do to improve your environment.

<u>Develop clear personal boundaries</u>: You need space in your environment where you are not bothered by other people's negative or unhelpful messages. You can create this space by your **words** and **actions.** It's okay to tell people no, or that you've changed your mind. *And sometimes you're going to have to go even further.*

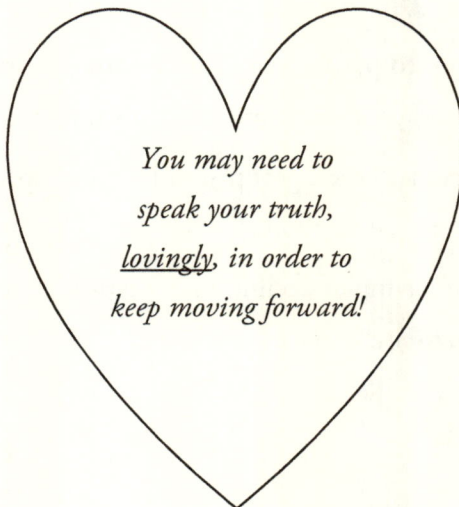

You may need to speak your truth, <u>lovingly</u>, in order to keep moving forward!

Here are just two examples of phrases you can use to create a healthy boundary for yourself:

> ➤ **When a conversation starts going downhill:** *Excuse me, I have some work I need to finish up.*

> ➤ **When you need to decline an invitation that will bring you around negative people:** *I really appreciate your invite, but I'm making some changes in my life, and I need to focus on staying positive.*

What are some additional scenarios and "come-backs" you can think of? (See the ROLE PLAY exercise below).

ROLE PLAY: Setting Personal Boundaries

This role-play exercise will allow everyone in the group to come up with their own role-play.

- ❖ Break up into partners of 2; if the number in the large group is uneven, then a single group of 3 is fine.
- ❖ Each person in each group should come up with an example of having to tell someon
- ❖ e "No" or having to decline an invitation, *or something else that requires setting a personal boundary.*

❖ The partners will role-play these scenarios with each other, each person having the opportunity to act out setting their boundary (i.e., saying no, declining, the invitation, etc.)

❖ Be sure to challenge each other a little bit, so that the person saying "No" has to be clear with the other person.

❖ Return to the large group and role-play one of these scenarios for the group.

Decide to meet new people: True friendships take time to develop, but you can still decide to be a little more outgoing and meet new people!

- Strike up conversations with people at work who you've observed being positive.

- Look for active "meet-up" groups online that are moving in the direction that you want to go! Meet-up groups aren't just support groups; they include book clubs, movie-going groups, photography bugs, bird watchers – you name it! Look for a group that is *doing* something that interests you!

- If you're on Facebook or other social media, look at your social media connections and consider if any of them are truly *positive* people. If you find some who are, reach out to them and start a conversation.

"Up" Your Self-Empowerment Game! That's right, your new environment needs to include positive media that educates and empowers you.

- ❖ Read short books about personal development.
- ❖ Search online for blogs, which are very short articles. In the search bar, type in "self-esteem blog" or "positive thinking blog."
- ❖ Follow these same steps for podcasts that you can listen to regularly.
- ❖ Watch TV or Netflix documentaries about people who overcame huge obstacles in their lives: athletes, entertainers, Civil Rights activists, and so many others! Let their stories inspire you to keep moving forward.
- ❖ Simply take time to learn more about the world around you. Read travel magazines or go to travel websites, where you can see so much more than your everyday surroundings.

Decide whether you need a job change: Of course, you need to work and continue creating income for yourself, but begin looking at your work environment closely and decide whether this is an environment that you want to stay in. If you hate the work you do, strongly dislike the people you work with, and/or disagree with your employer's values and policies, now is a good time to open your mind about a job change.

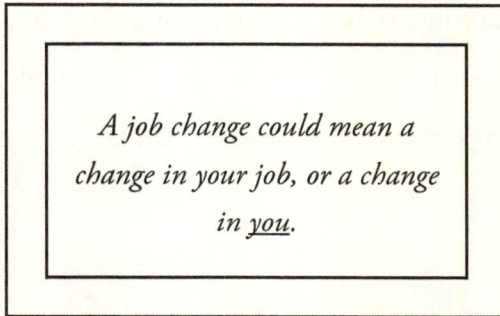

> *A job change could mean a change in your job, or a change in you.*

Before you make a change in your job, do these things:

> ➤ Look at what it is exactly that you hate about your job. Is there something you can change that would make your job more pleasant, such as delegate some work to others, get more organized yourself, or have an honest conversation with your boss about your ideas for addressing problems?

> ➤ If it's the people you dislike, can you interact with them differently, such as be more positive, more helpful, or more clear when you give them a task or when you need their help?

> ➤ If you disagree with your employer's way of doing business, are there suggestions you can make in your own department that may help you to feel more positive about the work the company does?

Once you've done these things, if you still feel you need to change your work environment, then by all means, begin looking for a new job!

Be encouraged! You can absolutely change your personal environment so that you are surrounded – most of the time – by people, places, and media that will support your steps toward rebuilding yourself!

SUCCESS PRINCIPLE #8

Create an Accountability Team

～

Championship teams are built on being prepared, playing unselfishly, and being held accountable.

JASON KIDD

What does the word, **accountability** mean? It refers to taking responsibility for the various successes *and* failures you experience. Being accountable includes understanding that ultimately, **you**, and no one else, is responsible for your personal growth and success.

Let's look at two examples of being accountable. The second asks for your input:

1) Your boss gives you a project with a deadline. You decide to recruit a co-worker's help, but during the last week of the

project, this co-worker has been out sick for 3 days. Your boss will hold **you** accountable for completing the project on time. You may have to ask someone else to help you, or you may have to finish the entire project on your own. Your boss entrusted you with completing the project, and you accepted the task, so you are accountable for seeing it through – and no one else.

2) You borrowed $50 from your sister and told her you'd repay her on the 1st of next month. A week before the 1st, you have to get brake work done on your car, and this eats up all of your "leftover" money you were planning to use to repay your sister.

Do you believe, given the unexpected circumstances, that you are accountable to your sister for repaying the $50? Do you believe that your sister should forgive the debt, or hold you accountable for repaying it in full within a reasonable time frame?

You are Accountable for You!

Whether you think it's fair or unfair, you are accountable for your actions that may lead to success or failure. As you determine to rebuild your life, you will absolutely come across barriers and difficult circumstances – and these are obstacles that you must decide to overcome. Once you decide to keep moving forward, you will find ways to do just that.

Failure is allowed – blaming others is not!

Don't Excuse Yourself

We all experience failure. As you read earlier in this book, failure is an opportunity to learn and grow. But before you can learn from your failure, you have to own it as <u>your</u> failure, not anyone else's. So, it's okay to explain what happened, but if you make an excuse (i.e., *excuse yourself from being accountable*) by blaming someone or something else for your failure, you won't grow and will most likely continue to experience failure in that particular area.

Excuses hold you back in two ways:

1) When you make an excuse, you don't see the failure as your own, and so you cannot learn from it.

2) Making an excuse also excuses you (in your mind, anyway) from turning the mistake or failure into a success. If you don't think you did anything wrong, then you don't have to make it right. What a missed opportunity!

Accept Your Accountability and Move Forward!

While making excuses holds you back, accepting your accountability gives you the drive to do your best and work around obstacles that get in your way. You will feel more in control of your life, you'll go about setting goals more seriously, and you'll expect results of yourself.

CREATE YOUR ACCOUNTABILITY TEAM

You no doubt are aware that rebuilding your life after experiencing some devastation is serious business! The road gets tough, and so the best way to become and remain accountable is by forming an **accountability team.**

What is an Accountability Team?

An accountability team can be just a few people – 2 or 3 – who want to see you succeed *and who you want to see succeed.* That's right – in an accountability team, everyone keeps everyone else accountable! Teams like this are a great way for you to learn how to be accountable because you'll be keeping others accountable! The few people in an accountability team are committed to keeping each other accountable to the goals they have each set for themselves.

How Accountability Teams Work

Accountability team members decide how they want to keep each other accountable. This may be through sharing a set of goals that each person has. Members could then check-in on a regular basis that they decide upon, and then each person lets the team know if they reached their goal, and any obstacles they had to work around. Today's technology makes it easy to stay in touch with accountability team members – through phone, email, video chats, and group video sessions. Some groups may even want to set up their own social media platform where they can post messages to each other and chat whenever it's convenient!

Accountability teams are a great way to keep you from making excuses to yourself about why you didn't get something done! Team members will let you know when you're making an excuse or giving someone else credit, and they will help you to "own" your growth process.

Identify Your Team Members

Make a list of the people you know -- directly or indirectly through a friend or co-worker – who are "success-bound." These are the folks who are always busy getting things done, and who generally do well at whatever they do. They seem to feel good about themselves and have a positive attitude.

From your list, identify the people you know to be honest and who are not people-pleasers; you want to choose people who will be straight-up with you, not try to be your buddy or get on your good side. Reach out to these people via phone, email, or social media. Let them know two things:

1) You have set some personal/career goals for yourself, and you want a couple of folks to help keep you accountable.

2) You want them to be part of a small team where people keep each other accountable to the goals they set for themselves.

ROLE PLAY – Reaching Out to Your Accountability Team

Let's keep this simple:

- Choose a partner.

- Each of you role-play asking the other to be part of an accountability team.

(Note: Before you begin, think about what you want to say to the person; don't beg them!)

- Report back to the group about how you felt asking for this kind of help.

Commit to the Work of Your Accountability Team

Once you have a small team of people in place, don't be surprised if they rely on you to be the team leader because this was your idea! But that's great, right? You can let people know what an accountability team is all about, and then as a team you all can determine how often to connect.

If you do take the lead on your team, this means at minimum sending out a reminder to the group a few days ahead of your scheduled connection day and time. But if you want to be a little more ambitious, you can every now and then send out a motivational post to the group – it can be a quote or a very short personal story that you think will inspire or motivate others.

The most important thing you can do as a member of an accountability team is to **be accountable and stay accountable.** Just doing this will definitely move you forward – and you'll be setting a tremendous example for others to duplicate!

(Duplicate? Well, we'll talk more about that with Success Principle #10!)

GROUP DISCUSSION

➤ How do you think an accountability team can help you to move forward?

➤ Do you think there are any "down sides" to becoming part of an accountability team?

SUCCESS PRINCIPLE #9

Be Coachable

❧

My best skill was that I was coachable. I was a sponge and aggressive to learn.

MICHAEL JORDAN

We all know that the child who listens to and does what a coach advises is on the right path toward really learning the sport they're playing – and winning! Coaching is not just useful in sports, but is highly useful for anyone who's on the path toward making major changes in their life. This success principle is all about being coachable – ready, willing and able to receive instruction from someone who's already been where you're trying to get.

Do You <u>Need</u> to be Coached?

If you knew that someone was available and willing to help you rebuild your life, would it make sense for you to accept their help? You would probably say yes! But are you ready to receive that person's help? Before you can truly benefit from being coached, first learn to be humble.

What Does It Mean to be "Humble"?

You may be thinking that a humble person is also a weak person. Not so!

- A person who is humble has the following qualities:
- They are honest about their circumstances.
- They recognize that they don't have all the answers and are willing to learn from others.
- They are not prideful or boastful.
- They don't need recognition from others; they are content knowing they've done a good job.

These are strengths, not weaknesses. A humble person is one who can accept criticism and correction without being offended and blaming the coach! One who is humble is also willing to be held accountable for their actions.

Many athletes are quite humble. Usually, when a coach talks about one of his or her players being coachable, that player is also humble.

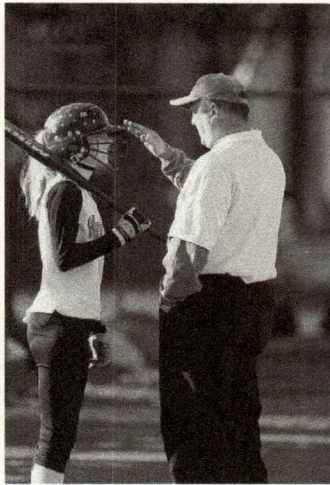

Being Humble in a "Hostile" World

Okay, so you may be thinking that being humble is great, but will people respect you when you're humble? If you're honest about the mistakes you've made in life, won't people jump on that as a way to put you down or deny you certain opportunities? Well, remember that Success Principle #3 focused on being careful who you share your success and failures with. Not everyone needs to know your history, so don't offer it to every listening ear! And generally, people will respect you when you admit you don't have all the answers – it actually makes you seem easier to relate to. In addition, people are attracted to someone who's confident, but not boastful. Your being humble will definitely be considered a great quality, even in today's competitive world.

Decide to Be Coachable!

Being (or becoming) a person who is coachable is key to your ability to press the "reset" button in your life, and to then follow through with all that is necessary to rebuild yourself. Whether you are rebounding from addiction, the loss of a loved one, betrayal, incarceration, business failure, or some other form of devastation, you must be coachable in order to receive what others have to offer you.

GROUP EXERCISE: Identify Who's READY to be Coached!

Read each statement below: Is that person ready to be coached or not?:

How are you going to tell me what I need to do? You've never been in prison before.

Ready ____   Not Ready _____

Why?_____

_____

_____

I have a good friend whose sister has some information she wants to share with me about grieving. I don't know if she's ever lost anyone, but I'll see what it is she wants to share.

Ready _____   Not Ready _____

Why?:_____

_____

_____

I really don't think I should expect anybody's help. I climbed down into this hole all by myself, so I can climb right back out of it on my own.

Ready _____Not Ready _____

Why?:_____

_____

_____

Look here, I need all the help I can get!

Ready ___ Not Ready ___

Why?:_____

_____

_____

If I have questions, I'm going to ask them. I won't keep them to myself.

Ready ___ Not Ready _____

Why?:_____

_____

_____

Informal and Formal Coaching Relationships

Before considering what to look for in a coach, know that a coach doesn't have to be someone you pay. There are plenty of people – either in your life already, or who you can make an effort to find – who will gladly offer encouragement, advice, and help keeping you on track toward regaining your life.

If you have the funds, a professional career coach may be the best option for you. These coaches are dedicated to helping you clarify your goals, outline the steps you need to take to reach your goals, and they'll hold you accountable.

Which kind of coach is best for you? Well, your wallet may be the determining factor. Just know that whether your coaching takes place in an office, your apartment, over a video call, a cup of coffee, or after a basketball game:

> *The most important part of coaching is your readiness to be coached!*

What to Look for in a Coach

What qualities should you look for in a coach, whether it's a friend of a friend, or a professional coach that you will be paying?

- ✓ **Experience** – You want to make sure that this person has a successful "track record" of helping others on their pathway toward a new life.

- ✓ **Sincerity** - This person has demonstrated that they are sincere. Even if you have not met them, they should in some way communicate that they genuinely care about your success.

- ✓ **Honesty** – You want someone who will give you honest feedback and hold you accountable to your goals.

✓ **Confidential** – Look for someone who knows how to keep your business private. This is especially true if you choose a coach who is a personal acquaintance.

✓ **Empathy** – Any coach needs to be able to walk a mile in your shoes. This person should not pity you, but have a true appreciation for your pain and struggle.

Finding Coaches

You may already have in mind someone (or more than one person) who would be an excellent coach for you. If this is not the case, is there someone you have observed that seems to carry themselves with confidence, someone who always has an encouraging word, someone who has gone through some struggles but has overcome them and is doing well?

You may find a number of coaches in a support group that you attend. Great! Coaching doesn't have to happen 1-on-1. You can receive coaching – wise counsel, encouragement, and correction – in a group setting. Just be sure that everyone in the group is sincerely interested in your progress.

Your coach may be a family member or close friend. As long as they are committed to being honest and straight-forward with you, and that they will keep your conversations confidential.

Finally, keep in mind that the people who end up being your coaches in life may surprise you: A coach may be your spouse, a co-worker, or a Facebook friend that you actually don't know that well, but contributes greatly to your positive mindset.

REMEMBER:

If you are coachable, you will be able to receive the wisdom and correction that will help you to move forward!

SUCCESS PRINCIPLE #10

Duplicate Success

❧

You can't duplicate success if you don't write the recipe down. —
TIM FARGO

The concept of duplication is pretty easy to understand: take something and repeat it, in the exact same way, to get the exact same outcome. Duplicating success is a smart and efficient way to find your own success and to help others succeed as well.

Examples of Duplication in Business

The best example of the duplication principle in business is the franchise business. When you visit a fast food franchise in Atlanta, you know that you can visit that same franchise in Chicago and your sandwich and French fries will taste exactly the same. This is because

all of the machinery, food suppliers, and processes in a franchise are the same – down to how many seconds the fries stay in the hot grease!

Examples of Duplication in Life

Identical twins are certainly an example of duplication in life. In many respects, twins are distinctly unique human beings, but some look so much alike that we cannot tell them apart. When you duplicate someone – or they duplicate you – you remain your unique self, but your success looks very similar!

Social media sharing is another way that people duplicate the ideas, advice, and actions of others. With a simple click, a video or tweet can go viral – millions of people will be watching and responding to the same information.

Success Can be Duplicated!

You are unique, and you could even argue that your circumstances are also unique. However, the principles that will guide you as you rebuild your life are the same, regardless of the specific devastation you have experienced.

The 11 success principles in this book are tried and true! Successful people from all walks of life have allowed these principles to steer them into new territory where they gain the confidence to make new choices and live a more fulfilled life. These success principles make it possible for you to duplicate their success. This doesn't mean that you will succeed in the exact same manner; it means that you will experience positive growth and change in the direction you want to go.

And of course, you also have the opportunity to help others duplicate your success! Committing yourself to the success principles will help you to experience how the principles actually work to spur your growth. You will gain confidence in their effectiveness – and you will *want* to see others duplicate your success!

Duplication is all about keeping the ball rolling!

Who Can Benefit from Your Success?

By committing yourself to the success principles in this book, you are duplicating someone's success. Who do you know that would benefit from *your* success?

You may not feel ready to mentor or coach someone, but you can pass along these success principles to others who are in need of making significant life changes for the positive. Don't be shy about sharing what you know. Instead, envision their success. Then express gratitude that you are in a position to help others to change their lives, and open yourself to the opportunity to benefit them!

IMPORTANT: Duplicate your success only when you have experienced some levels of success yourself, <u>and</u> you feel confident enough to share your success with others!

How Exactly Do You Duplicate Your Success?

Here are some things that you can do to begin duplicating your own success:

- ➤ **Think carefully about who in your life may need support**. This could be a family member, friend, associate, or co-worker.

- ➤ **Take some time to observe this person** and consider whether you think they are open to your support. Have they said or done anything to make you think they would welcome or reject your offer of support? Pay attention to these verbal and nonverbal cues.

- ➤ **Talk with the person**. Simply ask them, *So what's going on? How have you been?* Engage in honest conversation with them over a period of time to build their trust.

- ➤ **Empathize.** Let the person know, *I went through some real tough things, not exactly like what you're going through, but close.* And then share with them your story, or parts of it.

- ➤ **Let them know the steps you've taken to change your life.**

- ➤ **Offer your ongoing support.** Be careful not to over-commit yourself. Offer support that you can make good on. It may be sitting down for coffee once a week, or a phone call once or twice a week, a weekly game of chess, or a check-in via social media.

- ➤ **Commit yourself to seeing this person through to their success.** Your level of support can decrease over time – for example, you may both decide that checking in monthly rather than weekly is fine. Still, unless this person tells you otherwise, *stay connected with them.* Continue to encourage them, and you may want to offer them your own stories of how you overcame circumstances. Buy most importantly, keep referring them to the same success principles that helped you. **You may not be able to counsel this person, but you can always direct them to helpful success principles!**

GROUP DISCUSSION

➤ Which success principles have been most meaningful and helpful to you thus far?

➤ Even though the 11 success principles in this book come as a "package," is there **one** principle that you think is most fitting for:

- Someone who lost their life savings

- A recovering addict

- Someone who was incarcerated

- Someone who lost a loved one

- Someone betrayed by a spouse

SUCCESS PRINCIPLE #11

Sow Good Seeds: If I Could Turn Back the Hands of Time

~

It's better to look ahead and prepare, than to look back and regret.

JACKIE-JOYNER KERSEE

The two words that we hear most often spoken by people who have regrets are, "If only." But those words are unhelpful because they don't move you forward, and in fact, they can slow down your progress or even stop you in your tracks. Knowing better today than you did yesterday is called growth. Instead of listing your regrets, express your gratitude that you are in a different place and can see where you made mistakes.

Forgive Yourself and Others

In order to truly move forward and *keep* moving forward, you're going to have to forgive yourself for any decisions you made or actions you took that impacted yourself or others negatively. Forgiveness is like being in a courtroom in which the jury finds you (or others) guilty, but the judge declares that your sentence has already been served. You and others you hurt or who may have hurt you have all served your time – *now, demonstrate gratitude by moving forward!*

If you are struggling with forgiveness, seek counsel from a pastor or priest, or search for articles and books to read about forgiveness by doing a Google search for *how to forgive.*

SMALL GROUP DISCUSSION

In groups of 3-4 people, take about 30 minutes to share your answers to the following 2 questions. **Keep people's names confidential:**

What is one thing that you need to forgive yourself for?

Who is one person that you need to forgive?

How will forgiving that person help you to move forward?

Grab Hold of Your New Attitude!

Forgiveness allows you to adopt a new attitude:

I'M MOVING FORWARD!

NO BITTERNESS & NO

This new attitude will not come to you magically overnight. You will walk through much to reach this level of freedom, but you **will** reach it as you continually let go of old, negative ways of thinking about yourself and walk according to what's true about you – i.e., your desire to grow and change, your strengths, and your commitment to your dreams and goals.

Time to Sow Some Seeds!

The word "sow" is another word for "plant," as in planting seeds. You have taken in much information – and hopefully motivation and inspiration – by reading through this workbook. Many seeds have been planted in your conscience regarding how to think about yourself, how to keep hold of your dreams, how to create an environment in which you can thrive, and other important principles about successfully rebuilding your life.

Now it's your turn to sow some seeds. You can choose to sow "bad" seeds – seeds that will not grow into anything helpful to yourself or others. Sowing bad seeds includes complaining to others about your problems, making excuses about why you didn't keep your word, negative self-talk, and regrets. Or, you can sow "good" seeds that will produce success. Good seeds include sharing your positive mindset and success principles with others, being accountable to others for your actions, and forgiving yourself and those who have harmed you.

Let's Examine the Soil

So, where will you plant your good seeds? This question is important, because even the best seeds will not produce if the soil is not adequate for growing things. Not always, but oftentimes you will have the opportunity to choose the type of soil you sow your seeds in. For instance, you won't want to share your dream with a negative naysayer, or with a gossiper who may widely share your personal dream or story with anyone they meet. No, you'll want to share your journey or your dream with someone who has demonstrated their love, support, and encouragement. You may also choose to share some success principles with someone who sincerely wants to change their life around, but doesn't know how or where to begin. This type of "soil" – i.e., an open heart – is the <u>best</u> type of soil in which to sow your good seed!

GROUP DISCUSSION

➤ What are some negative outcomes of sowing bad seed?

➤ What are some of the benefits of sowing good seed?

<u>MINDSET SELF-SURVEY #2</u>

This short survey will help you to become more aware of what you believe about yourself, **today, at this moment.** Compare your answers to this Mindset Self-Survey with the same answers to Mindset Self-Survey #1, featured in Success Principle #1 of this workbook.

Circle the best answer for each statement. (Note: This survey is your personal information; share it with others only if you choose to do so.)

1. The way I was raised as a child is a major reason why I now need to rebuild my life.

Strongly agree Slightly agree Slightly disagree Strongly disagree

Comments(optional):

_____

_____

_____

2. My circumstance (being an addict, betrayed, unemployed, incarcerated, a survivor, or other devastating circumstance) has put a limit on what I can achieve in society.

Strongly agree Slightly agree Slightly disagree Strongly disagree

Comments(optional):

_____

_____

_____

3. My lack of education and skill will hold me back as I rebuild my life.

Strongly agree Slightly agree Slightly disagree Strongly disagree

Comments(optional):

_____

_____

_____

4. In order for me to succeed, I must succeed on my own; no one can really help me.

Strongly agree Slightly agree Slightly disagree Strongly disagree

Comments(optional):

_____

_____

_____

5. I have a great amount of control over my future.

Strongly agree Slightly agree Slightly disagree Strongly disagree

Comments(optional):

_____

_____

_____

6. I know what my passion is.

Strongly agree Slightly agree Slightly disagree Strongly disagree

Comment(optional):

_____

_____

_____

7. I have clear goals for what I want to achieve in the next 5 years.

Strongly agree Slightly agree Slightly disagree Strongly disagree

Comments(optional):

_____

_____

_____

8. A lot of other people deserve success more than I do.

Strongly agree Slightly agree Slightly disagree Strongly disagree

Comments(optional):

_____

_____

_____

9. The present is not as important as the future.

Strongly agree Slightly agree Slightly disagree Strongly disagree

Comments(optional):

_____

_____

_____

10. In order to succeed, I need money more than anything else.

Strongly agree Slightly agree Slightly disagree Strongly disagree

Comments(optional):

_____

_____

_____

CONGRATULATIONS!

You have completed your study of 11 success principles that will help you to rebuild your life! Hopefully by now you have a clear vision for your future, and you have set some goals that will help you to make your vision a reality.

Remember that you are **not** alone! If you do feel alone, you can look for help and encouragement by searching online for nonprofit organizations and meet-up groups that specialize in your area of need. If you don't have a computer, go to your local library and ask a librarian to help you find the kind of support you seek. Know that you are on the path to becoming your best self!

MUCH CONTINUED SUCCESS TO YOU!

ABOUT THE AUTHOR

As an educator, retired law enforcement professional, author, and businesswoman, Dr. R. Renee Dupree has risen to national prominence by delivering a high quality of service, along with messages of hope and positive energy to the community, her clients and friends. Her message tells people how to lift each other up, speak victory into their own lives, be the president of their fan club, and shake off doubt and despair. It is a message Dr. Dupree has learned from her own life and one she is helping others apply to their lives.

Born in Brooklyn, New York, Dr. Dupree is one of five children born to hard working, southern-born parents who instilled a work ethic in their children that has served as the driving force behind who Dr. Dupree is today.

As one of the industry's most energetic and positive motivational speakers, Dr. Dupree presents to organizations throughout the United

States with a "heart-felt" style and tremendous passion. She leaves her audiences with a larger vision for their lives and the motivation to take the next step to getting their lives on track and living their dream.